The Road to the Briar Patch
The Childhood of Joel Chandler Harris

By Chloe Abigail Shelton

Copyright ©2016 Chloe Abigail Shelton
Pickles and Popcorn Press

All rights reserved including the right of reproduction in whole or in part in any form.

Cover Design, Texts and Illustrations: Copyright ©2016 by Chloe Abigail Shelton

Includes biographical references.
Summary: A fictionalized biography concentrating on the boyhood of the author of the Uncle Remus Stories based, in part, on first and second hand accounts.

For more information about Pickles and Popcorn Press or other works related to this book, please visit www.PencilsAndPixieDust.com

ISBN-13: 978-1530257720
ISBN-10: 1530257727

Author's Note

The Road to the Briar Patch is the culmination of more than a year-long study of Joel Chandler Harris. My own road to the Briar Patch started out with an admiration of Walt Disney and a love of family vacations to Walt Disney World.

Inspired by Walt Disney World and the popular attraction, Splash Mountain, I began to study the history of the ride for my educational and entertainment website, "PencilsAndPixieDust.com."

My studies led me to my own discovery of the controversial movie, "Song of the South" as well as other little-known works of literature and film.

I dedicate this book to all of the dreamers and doers like Walt Disney and Joel Chandler Harris. May you always find the courage to try!

Psalm 37:4

TABLE OF CONTENTS

EATONTON FAMILY AND FRIENDS...v

FORWARD...vii

INTRODUCTION...viii

CHAPTER ONE: A NEW FRIEND...1

CHAPTER TWO: RABBIT HUNTIN'..10

CHAPTER THREE: THE ACADEMY..12

CHAPTER FOUR: THE GULLY MINSTRELS................................15

CHAPTER FIVE: THE PRINTER'S DEVIL..................................18

CHAPTER SIX: TURNWOLD...22

TURNWOLD PLANTATION FRIENDS.......................................28

CHAPTER SEVEN: SETTLING IN...37

CHAPTER EIGHT: A NEW DISCOVERY....................................47

CHAPTER NINE: A BIG STEP..58

CHAPTER TEN: A CELEBRATION...68

EPILOGUE: MAY 9, 1865..78

DEEPER IN THE BRIAR PATCH..82

ABOUT THE AUTHOR..83

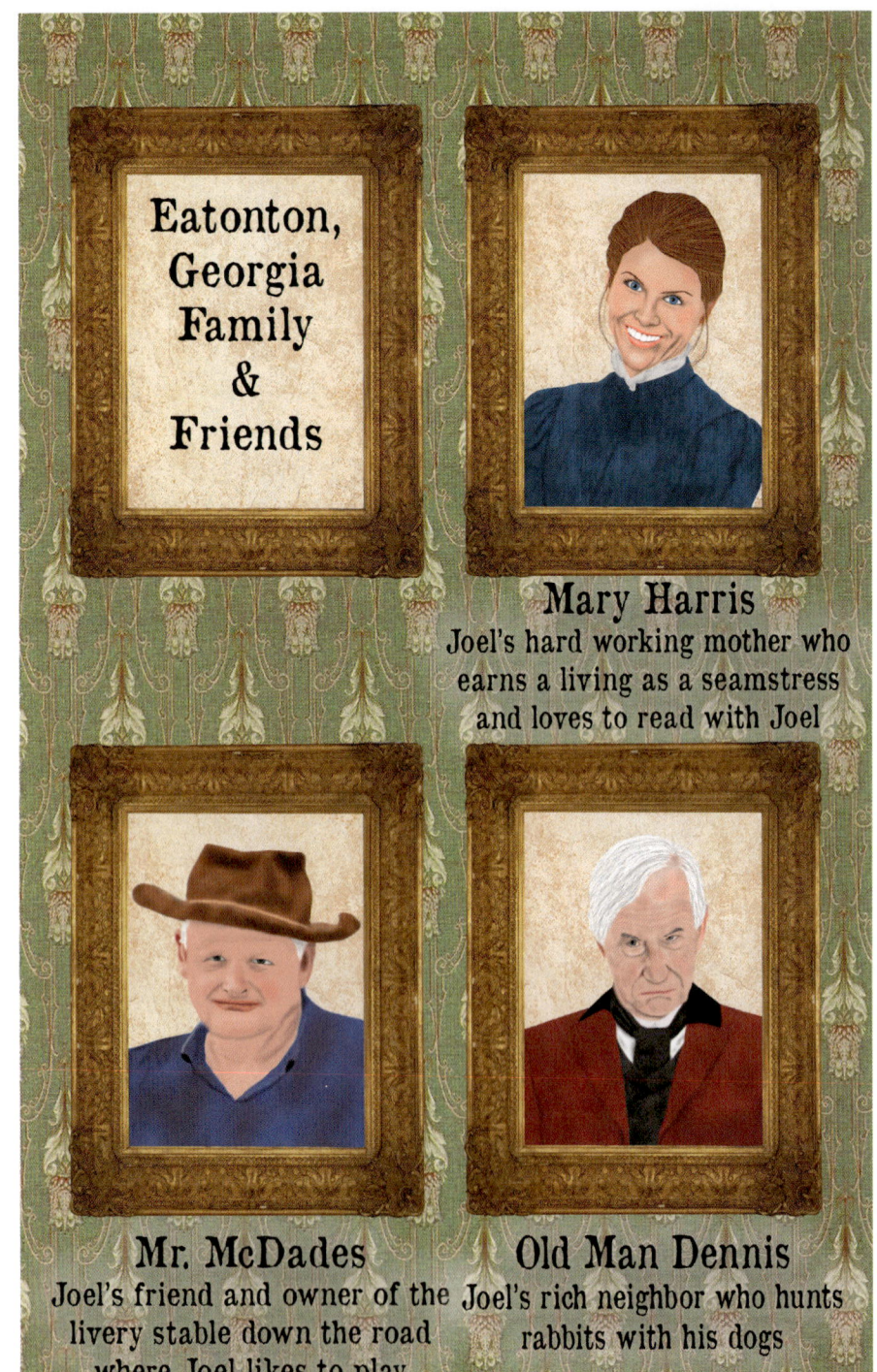

Aunt Betsy Cuthbert
Joel's neighbor and Toby's grandmother who makes the best ginger cakes in town

C.D. Lawrance
Joel's new friend who just moved to Eatonton, Georgia

Toby Cuthbert
Joel's good friend and partner in crime

Hut Adams
Joel and C.D's friend from school who is four years older than them

FORWARD

This is the story of a young boy and the family that raised him. His unlikely family included slaves and former slaves, a plantation owner and a gruff Irish printer.

Joel Chandler Harris came to inspire people such as President Theodore Roosevelt, who said that Harris provided the "best contribution to literature this side of the ocean" and "Presidents may come and presidents may go, but Uncle Remus stays put. Georgia has done a great many things for the Union, but she has never done more than when she gave Mr. Joel Chandler Harris to American literature."

Mark Twain called him "the oracle of the nation's nurseries."

He inspired Beatrix Potter, who got her start illustrating Brer Rabbit stories.

And, he inspired Walt Disney who called Harris' recorded stories "timeless," with "magnificent pictorial quality" and "rich and tolerant humor."

Harris was also a forward thinking progressive who said "The only ambition that I ever had, the only line of policy that I ever mapped out in my own mind" is to "finally dissipate all ill feelings and prejudices that now exist between the races."

Joel Chandler Harris began writing down the Uncle Remus stories in order to "preserve in permanent shape those curious mementos of a period that will no doubt be sadly misrepresented by historians of the future."

This is the story of a boy and his family: a family of people who, together, shaped an insecure youngster into the man he became.

Introduction

"Now, this here tale didn't just happen yesterday, nor the day before. No! It was a long time ago. The critters: they was closer to the folks. And the folk: they was closer to the critters. And if you'll s'cuse me for saying so, it was better all around."

Joel sat wide eyed in wonder. Every night when he came to listen to stories, they started something like that. He knew exactly what was to come: Brer Fox would get hungry for some rabbit, but he would never get it, for his nemesis, Brer Rabbit was the most cunning and quick-witted rabbit in the whole state of Georgia!

Uncle George's gentle words danced gracefully through the fire-lit cabin, until they reached Joel's eager ears.

Sometimes, when Joel was feeling particularly shy, he would pretend to be Brer Rabbit and outwit his Brer Fox.

Sometimes his "Brer Fox" would be his friends from back home, and sometimes "Brer Fox" would be his boss at the newspaper. Whomever it was, Joel always felt better pretending to be someone else. And Brer Rabbit was his favorite character to be.

Uncle George filled the cabin with one of Joel's favorite stories: "Brer Rabbit and the Peanut Patch."

Joel longed for this moment in Uncle George's Cabin to go on forever. Little did he know that he would be the one who made that happen.

And, little did he know that he would form a legacy that began with a shy boy from Georgia, and would lead to one of the most well known media conglomerates of all time.

This is the story of Joel Chandler Harris.

STOP! READ THIS FIRST!

The word "slave" is used in this story to clarify some of the characters' place in society. However, that word did not define them. They were individuals with gifts, talents, good traits and not-so-good traits. Each of them had a story to tell and guidance for Joel.

Dialect is used here for all of the characters, not to further a stereotype, but to better tell the story.

Chapter One

1855

A NEW FRIEND

"Joel! Joel Harris, where are you?" Her words echoed like church bells.

"Coming, Mama!" Joel pulled the knot on the bucket one more time to make sure it was tight, then oh, so carefully, he lifted the bucket over the side of the loft. He yanked the rope to make sure it wouldn't fall.

"You get out here this instant or I will come get you myself!"

A rush of panic ran through him. If she so much as touched that stall...

"No! Don't..." Joel began. He was cut off by Mr. McDades walking in to the livery stable to join Joel's mother.

"I wouldn't go over there if I was you" Mr. McDades warned Joel's mother.

"I'm looking for my son. I'm sure he's in here" she replied

"Oh, he's in here, all right." He pointed toward the loft.

Joel got as low as he could.

"Been there all day" McDades continued. "I saw him haul a bucket o' tar up there. I think he rigged it."

"Then, why in *this world* did you not stop him?" she asked.

"Well, ma'am, it's always a good laugh when someone gets it!"

Mr. McDades reached down, picked up a rock, and threw it at the nearest stall. The door swung in and tar poured down on the dirt floor.

Joel couldn't help but release a cackle when he saw his Mama's face. Mr. McDades was laughing so hard that his face had turned a bright, cherry red.

"Joel! You could have made a mess of me!" his mother reprimanded.

Joel started climbing down the ladder.

"Sorry, Mama" Joel said sheepishly.

"Young man, you will clean up every bit of tar in this here barn, or no book for a week!"

His mother looked sick.

A New Friend

"Never you mind that, Mrs. Harris" said Mr. McDades. "Ben can do that a lot quicker than little Joel. Besides, that's a very small price to pay for a laugh that good. What do you say, Joel?"

"Thank you, Mr. McDades!" Joel turned towards his mother and gave her a big hug.

"Seven year old boys shouldn't be playing with tar, Joel" his mother said in a more soothing tone.

Joel hugged her a little tighter as if to reassure her of his regret and she squeezed him back.

"We need to get home, now" Mrs. Harris said. "We have new neighbors and they have a boy about your age! He's excited to meet you and we've kept them waiting long enough."

They said goodbye to Mr. McDades and thanked him again for cleaning up the mess. Then, they hurried home.

They walked down the street and came across a large mansion. This was the house of Andrew Reid, the wealthiest man in Putnam County.

Mr. Reid had taken pity on Mary Harris after Joel's father left them shortly after Joel was born.

The Road to the Briar Patch

Joel's father was an Irishman with a major lack of ambition. He realized upon Joel's birth, that he would never be accepted by Mary's intelligent and well-loved family. So, he left, never to return.

Mr. Reid knew that Miss Mary was one of the smartest and sweetest ladies in all of Eatonton, and like everyone else in the little village, he wanted her as a neighbor. So, he offered her the use of his guest house as a home for her and little Joel.

Joel ran ahead as they turned toward the house. He ran through the grass and around the estate until he reached the little, white cottage in the garden. As he ran, he tossed his tar-stained coat over the clothes line.

He burst through the door to find a little family in the sitting room: a mama, a daddy, and two little boys. And, the older one looked about his age! A moment later his mother opened the door and stepped inside.

"There you are, Mary!" the lady said. "And, this must be

Joel!

"So sorry that took so long! Joel had a little mess. I must admit, he isn't the cleanest boy in Putnam County, but he's a *good* boy. He's my little garden helper" said Mary Harris.

"Oh! Isn't he darlin'?! I could just eat you up!" said the woman in a sing-songy voice.

Joel hated it when his mother's friends cooed over him. But, when he thought of all the pranks he would play on them, he felt better.

"Joel," his mother said "this is C.D. and Jim Lawrence. C.D. is 6 years old: close to your age! They just moved here. They need someone to show them around Eatonton."

"I sure do know my way around..." Joel said, staring at his Mother's prized hooked rug on the floor.

"Good! It's settled then! Why don't you three run along." Mary Harris patted her son on the cheek.

"Actually, Jim just got over a fever, but C.D. may go." Mrs. Lawrence pulled Jim over to her.

"Alright! You two, have fun!" Mrs. Harris nudged them out. As the door swung shut, they stood in an awkward silence for some time.

The Road to the Briar Patch

"So, what d'ya do for fun 'round here?" C.D. eventually asked.

Joel kicked the dirt around his feet.

"Same as anywhere else I s'pose..."

"Come on! There must be somethin'!"

An idea struck Joel's head.

"Okay. But we'll need s'more players. Come on!"

The two ran as fast as they could, with Joel in the lead. They ran all through town until they reached a small house. There, a little, old lady with dark skin was busy sweeping the front porch.

"S'cuse me, Aunt Betsy" said Joel politely. "We was wonderin' if Toby can come out and play."

The lady smiled.

"And, who is this dapper feller?" she asked.

"This is C.D.. He just moved here and I was showin' him

'round. I thought Toby might like to help me!" Joel took a step towards her in a familiar way.

"Alright. S'long as you stay for ginger-cakes, first" Aunt Betsy said as she turned and went inside the house to fetch her grandson.

"We're gonna be in so much trouble!" said C.D. "I ain't s'pose to talk to slaves!'

"Aunt Betsy ain't a slave! She's free! And she ain't my aunt, neither. Everybody just calls her 'Aunt.'" Joel was a little mad at C.D. for talking about Aunt Betsy like that, but he knew once he tried her ginger-cakes, all would be well again.

After eating ginger-cakes, the boys were on their way, once more, with the addition of Toby.

"So, where we headed?" asked Toby.

"Ol' Man Dennis' barley patch" Joel replied. "...to play hide-and-seek."

"Hide-and-seek? Oh, boy!" C.D. said excitedly.

"Are you crazy, Joe Harris?" scolded Toby, using Joel's

nickname. "Ol' Man Dennis will put 'is hounds on us if he spots us!"

"You don't have to come," Joel said "...if you're too scared!"

"I ain't scared! Why would I be scared?" Toby started walking faster. "Come on! Ain't you comin'?"

When they reached the barley patch, they drew straws and it was determined that C.D. was "it."

"I feel like I'm a tick standin' in somebody's hair!" C.D. looked enchanted. "I hope you two can hide as good as ticks! I'm gonna start countin'! One, two, three..."

Toby and Joel ran into the barley patch and ducked down to hide.

"Ready or not! Here I come!"

The days passed and soon Joel and C.D. were the best of friends. They did all sorts of things together.

One of Joel's favorite times of the week was Sunday morning when he would go to the basement of the Girl's Academy to attend Sunday School. C.D. had never been to a Sunday School before, so Joel started bringing him along every week.

And when school started, they took classes together at Miss Kate Davidson's mixed school for boys and girls. Although they didn't always show up for class.

Chapter Two

1856
RABBIT HUNTIN'

The school bell rang loudly throughout the village. But, Joel and C.D. couldn't care less. They ran as hard and as fast as they could. Their destination was the livery stable where they climbed the rickety wooden ladder and plopped down in the loft.

"What are we goin' to do, now?" Joel asked "We skipped school! We can't go home yet!"

"Good thing I thought'a that already!" said C.D., proudly. "We'ze going rabbit huntin'!"

"But my ol' hound, Brute's at home!" Joel said. "Ohhh!" He understood. "Lets go!"

They climbed down quickly and ran to Old Man Dennis' backyard where they stood at the edge of the woods and squawked and squawed, trying to attract the dogs.

All of his hunting dogs came running. The boys tied

ropes to the dogs' collars, and then off they all went into the woods to hunt some rabbit.

Four hours, two miles and five rabbits later, back in town, Mr. Harvey Dennis came home to discover all eight of his dogs were missing.

"My dogs are gone again with them boys" he said calmly. He mounted his horse and rode until he found C.D. and Joel.

"Boys, you've got my dogs, again" Old Man Dennis said simply.

Eight year old Joel held a rabbit up by its ears and smiled. The kids laughed, nervously.

"Do ya want a rabbit, Mr. Dennis?" Joel asked politely.

"I suppose we're all having rabbit stew for supper!" said Mr. Dennis, his gruff exterior turning to glee at the ingenuity of the young boys.

Joel and C.D. had plenty of adventures, but before long, Joel's head outgrew Miss Kate's classroom. And new adventures were underway.

Chapter Three

1858

THE ACADEMY

Joel and his mother lived in a cottage behind the mansion of the wealthy Mr. Andrew Reid. Mr. Reid generously paid for Joel to go to school at Eatonville School for Boys after Miss Kate's school stopped challenging him.

"Stand still!" said Mrs. Harris. "Let me finish hemming your sleeve!"

"But, C.D. will be here any minute, Ma!" Joel replied.

"So, he will. And you will look nice when he gets here!"

Just then, there was a knock on the door.

"He's here! Love ya, Mama!"

He kissed his mother's cheek, and then flew out the door.

"Hi, Joe!" said C.D. "Are ya ready?"

"Yep! Onward! To your first day of Academy!" said Joel, trying to impersonate a general in the army.

The Road to the Briar Patch

They started walking.

"Were you this nervous on *your* first day of Academy?" C.D. asked.

"Yes, but you'll be fine! *You* have *me*!"

"Yeah! Let's go!"

The school day came and went and Joel and C.D. were starting home when a boy, who looked several years older than them, walked up.

"Hello, Joe!" said the boy.

"Hello, Hut!" Joel responded.

"Who's your friend?" Hut asked.

"Oh, this is C.D.!" Joel turned to his friend. "C.D., this is Hut!"

"Hi!" said the bigger boy, with a friendly smile.

"What d' ya say to me walkin' home with ya?" asked Hut.

"Sure thing!" said Joel, happy to have his older friend join in.

And, they set off back into town, just as they would do the next day, and the next one, for years to come.

The Academy

Very soon, Joel, C.D. and Hut began to consider themselves the "Famous Trio" of Eatonton, Georgia.

Everyday they walked down Main Street to get to school. On the way home, they took a shortcut through Edmond Reid's watermelon patch and peach orchard.

Often, as they ran past the watermelons and peaches, they would try to snatch some of the sweet smelling fruit.

Ever so often, Mr. Reid would stand on his back porch and laugh quietly to himself as Joel and his friends ran away squat-legged, dropping fruit as they went, thinking that they had gotten away with high crimes, but instead, being secretly found out.

Chapter Four

THE GULLY MINSTRELS

Summer break arrived, and the Famous Trio was bored as could be. They sat around all day in the livery stable loft. Joel read books, C.D. weaved straw and Hut spent his days running his handkerchief though his fingers. (Joel found this strange, as neither he nor C.D. owned a handkerchief).

One day, as they were out at the creek getting some fresh air and fishing for minnows with Hut's handkerchief, Hut was struck with an idea.

"We'll have a circus!" he proclaimed proudly.

"But, where will we have it?" Joel asked.

"At the white mud gullies, of course!" Hut had evidently thought this through at one time or another.

"We have to charge for admission! To see talent such as ours should never be free!" C.D. said with a smile.

"Ma always needs pins for her sewing! We could charge pins!" Joel said.

"Good idea! How about ten pins to watch the show?" Hut was excited now. A profit was a profit whether it was money or pins.

Within an hour they had set up a little stage in the gully. At the top of the gully next to Aunt Betsy's house, they put a ticket booth, complete with a box in which to collect the pins.

Joel painted a sign to hang on the booth that said "Gully Minstrels: 10 pins for admittance" and included a picture of them on the stage.

Hut declared himself "The Boss." Joel was "The Funny Man." And C.D. was "The Treasurer."

Toby (who got in at the discounted price of five pins since it was in *his* backyard) told everyone far and wide about the gully minstrels.

And soon, kids from all around Putnam County poured in.

C.D. sat at his little ticket booth and took pins from the

The Road to the Briar Patch

children as they entered.

Hut welcomed everyone with a tip of his father's topper and a wave of his hankie.

Joel stood aside with a painted 'white mud' smile on his face, and waited for the show to begin.

After two full weeks of "mud gully minstrels" the trio decided to retire.

Every kid in Putnam County had seen the show...some more than once...and they were more famous than ever! But it was starting to feel like work, so they put their circus days behind them.

As for the pins, every day after the show Joel would bring his mother a handful of them and she would give him a hug, thank him dearly, and tell him how helpful he was being. But, after a couple days of this, she had no more need for any extra pins. By the end of the two weeks they had a box of pins and no use for them.

So ended the adventures of the "gully minstrels."

Chapter Five

1862

THE PRINTER'S DEVIL

The years passed and Joel's love for reading and writing only grew.

He spent his days reading with his mother or writing poems and short stories.

He knew he wanted to become a journalist. But Eatonton had no newspaper office at which he could get an apprenticeship.

Hut had gone off to boarding school, and C.D. was a blacksmith's apprentice. Joel knew it was his turn to do something more.

As he grew, his shyness began to overtake him. He spent more time with books than with people. And it seemed to bother him more when someone mocked his red hair or freckles.

He still loved to visit Toby and Aunt Betsy, but lately, he found himself in the post office more often than not. Newspaper subscriptions cost more than Joel and his mother could afford. The post master, a friend of Joel's, allowed him to read the papers before they were picked up by the subscribers. He loved to sit on a barrel and read the newspapers everyday when they came in.

One day in early Summer as he thumbed through the newspapers he noticed a new volume called *The Countryman*.

Then, to his surprise, he saw that the publisher was Joseph Addison Turner! Joel's mother frequently made Mr. Turner's clothes!

As he flipped though the paper he noticed a small ad in one corner:

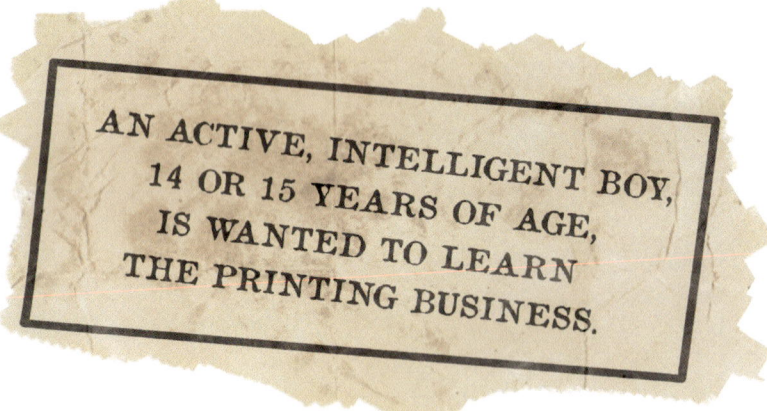

Joel ran home as fast as he could to tell his mother this news.

"But Joel!" his mother said. "The ad says fourteen or fifteen years old, and you're only thirteen!"

"But, it's worth a try, isn't it?" Joel couldn't believe his mother protested! "I'll write him and if he says no, then I'll find something here. But I can't just give up because I'm four months too young!"

She sighed. " I see you're determined and I won't stand in your way. I trust Mr. Turner and I know he'll do what's right."

"Thank you, Mama!" Joel lunged at his mother with a big bear hug. "I'll write to him right away!"

The days passed with no reply. Joel began to get worried.

One day, Joel was sitting at the post office reading a paper when he heard a commotion outside. A large carriage was coming through the town and stopped in front of Mr. Reid's mansion.

Joel immediately recognized it as the carriage of Mr. Turner! He dropped his paper and ran to his little house as quickly as he could. He burst though the door and ran into

Mr. Turner! His Mother gave him a little smile, and at that moment he knew his life had changed forever.

That very same day, Joel packed some clothes in his grandmother's old-fashioned trunk, gave his mother a kiss and boarded the carriage to his new life. Joel hated leaving his Mother but he knew that if he worked hard enough, he might eventually get paid. And, then he would be able to send her money to help care for her as she'd always done for him.

Chapter Six

TURNWOLD

The ride was long and tiresome. He couldn't help but think he would have to travel the lengthy nine miles if he wanted to see his mother or friends.

The carriage sped down a long lane with big, tall oaks on either side. Joel couldn't help but stick his head out the window and watch as the gigantic trees raced by.

Suddenly, the carriage was engulfed in a dense forest of tall oaks, hickories and other Georgian trees. The little grove was beautiful. Joel looked upon the big trees, enamored. The afternoon sun shown through them like the candles on his mother's Christmas tree.

Mr. Turner, who was seated next to him in the carriage, noticed Joel's interest in the grove.

"I see you like my little, enchanted forest" he said.

"Yes, sir! It's real pretty" Joel said shyly. He wanted to

make the best, possible impression on his new boss.

"When I moved here, years ago, with my younger brother, William, there were no trees. I hated it. Back in Dinwittie, Virginia where I'm from, there are trees everywhere! But, not here. Just acres of cotton and tobacco.

"So, I called on a man by the name of Andrew Jackson Downing. He was a well-known landscape gardener that sometimes worked near my hometown. Mr. Downing planned out the landscape of Turnwold.

"I asked him for a paradise, and I believe that is what he gave me. Would you agree?"

"Yes! It's beautiful!" Joel suddenly heard the sound of angry hawks overhead. He cringed slightly at the thought of the large, boisterous birds in the trees above the rocking carriage.

"In the many years since Mr. Downing helped me plan out my plantation's landscape, I'm afraid it grew somewhat, more compact. William has attempted to sway me to thin it out, but I did not plant this forest to chop it down! I intend to let it flourish! But, it does warrant some unwanted wildlife."

The Road to the Briar Patch

The carriage shook as a hawk landed on the wooden roof. Joel let out a yell in surprise and lunged back into his seat. Mr. Turner suddenly burst into uncontrollable laughter.

As Joel eased back into a normal sitting position, he too began to laugh. The two laughed the rest of the way down the lane in the midst of the little grove, rolling farmlands, and fragrant Bermuda grass meadows that stretched far off into the horizon.

The carriage suddenly halted in front of a big, white house. A man dressed in a fine livery opened the door of the carriage with a little bow. He set a box on the ground for Joel to step on. Joel exited the carriage with a smile and a nod toward the older man, Mr. Turner only steps behind him. He looked around in amazement. Turnwold was a grand plantation. There were acres of cotton fields, all being tended to by slaves. There was the big, white-washed house and other similarly painted buildings surrounding it. Big trees seemed to be everywhere he looked, making the whole plantation shady and quaint. Far off in the distance Joel could see a little group of log cabins that reminded him of a prairie town in books he'd read, although he knew the buildings made up the slave quarters.

"Now, Joel," said Mr. Turner "you will have a room in one of the "ells" of the big house. That's the 'L' shaped wing on the left side. Over there is the printing office. That is where you will work as the Printer's Devil. Down there is the slave quarters. You can go there if you'd like. Nowhere is off limits to you. But, please, try not to come into my study when I'm working."

Joel nodded fervidly.

"I hope you will start to think of Turnwold as your home."

"I will, sir!" Joel said with glee.

"Supper is at six. Don't be late! Now, go explore!"

He didn't hesitate. He ran as fast as he could to the first little cabin he saw.

Turnwold Plantation Friends

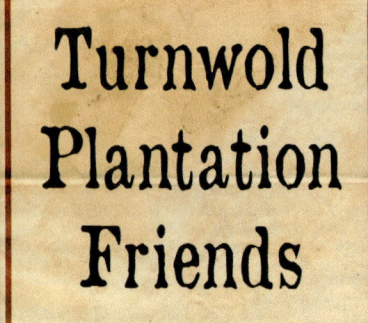

Joseph Addison Turner
The owner of Turnwold Plantation and editor of *The Countryman* newspaper

Ann "Wattie" Turner
The oldest child of Joseph Addison Turner

Willie Turner
Joel's mischievous friend and the younger brother of Wattie

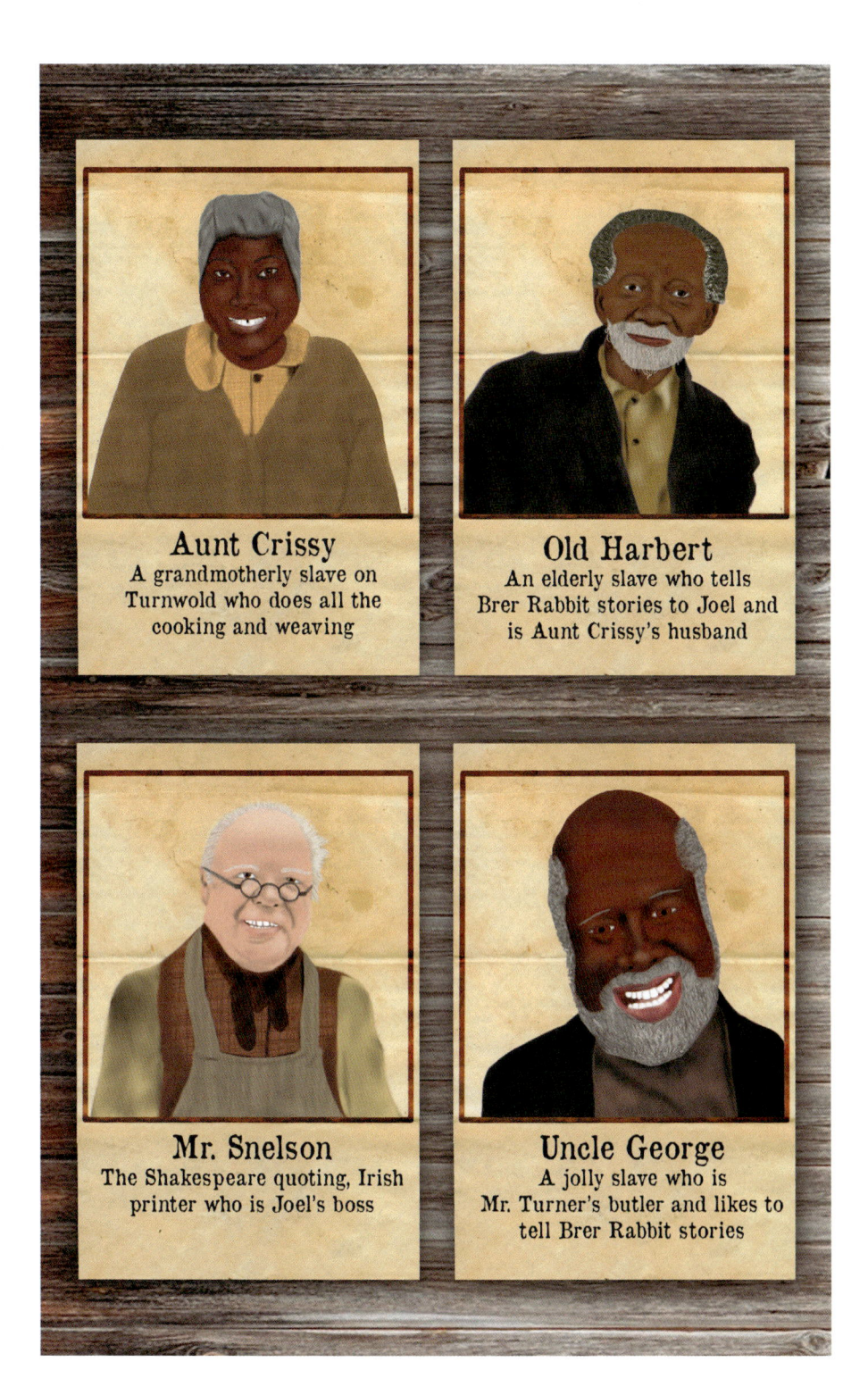

Aunt Crissy
A grandmotherly slave on Turnwold who does all the cooking and weaving

Old Harbert
An elderly slave who tells Brer Rabbit stories to Joel and is Aunt Crissy's husband

Mr. Snelson
The Shakespeare quoting, Irish printer who is Joel's boss

Uncle George
A jolly slave who is Mr. Turner's butler and likes to tell Brer Rabbit stories

Chapter Seven

SETTLING IN

Joel ran to what he knew was the printing office to see his new place of work. The office was a small cabin with a little porch on the front and a door on each end.

Joel walked in the front door and his mouth dropped open in awe. It was beautiful! He tentatively stepped towards the large old-fashioned hand press and stroked the side.

"A Washington No. 2!" Joel muttered as he read the side of the old machine. He could tell that it had seen better days, but despite its rust, Joel was in awe.

Settling In

He walked around the little stove in the center of the room to the desk where the Printer set the type. He grabbed a type box and a handful of letters out of the Printer's case and began to set type for a poem he had written. He wanted to see how fast he could lay the letters down.

"What are you doing with me printing stamps?" said a voice with a gruff, Irish accent, coming from behind him.

Joel turned to see Mr. Snelson. Mr. Turner had told him that Snelson was the Irishman he had hired as head printer. He was to be Joel's boss.

"I'm sorry. I was just seeing how fast I could lay the letters. You must be Mr. Snelson. Mr. Turner told me about you."

"That I am. You aren't the Printer's Devil, are ye?"

"Um...yes." Joel replied shyly.

"Well, I hope he intends to get me a second apprentice! I need a strong lad to help me run the press!"

"I can lay letters." Joel said sheepishly.

"Ay. Let me talk with Joseph." He trudged out the door and slammed it behind him. The door immediately swung open again.

"And don't *play* with me letters!" He slammed the door once more.

Joel was sad that the Printer didn't seem to like him, but he decided to just wait and see what Mr. Turner would say.

He walked around the small building that he would soon know so well and wondered if he had made the right decision. Joel went and sat next to the window and peered out. As he looked over the miles of endless cotton, he felt his stomach rumble. At that point he realized that he hadn't eaten lunch yet. He decided to go to the kitchen to see about some food.

He ran to the big house as fast as he could. As he ran he smelled the sweet aroma of the boxwood bushes that adorned the little path to the house. He ran past the Turnwold Family graveyard, covered with bright purple periwinkle. He walked up to the big front door and pushed it open. When the sight of the splendid interiors met his eyes, his jaw dropped in amazement. Besides the old doctor's house, he had never seen a more beautiful entryway! The ceiling stretched up so high that Joel thought it must be at least fifteen feet tall! The same older man that opened his carriage door earlier that day was busy at work inside. He sported a big, white, bushy beard and a dapper suit and was carefully wiping down a table in the grand hall.

"Ah, you mus be Marster Joe!" the old man said, walking up to him.

"Yes. What's your name?" The old man let out a laugh.

"You's want ta know *my* name?"

Joel nodded.

"George Terrell at your service. But you's can call me 'Uncle George'!"

"Nice to meet you, Uncle George! I was wondering where the kitchen is?"

"The kitchins' ain't in the house! It's outside and to da right. But, don't go spoilin' your supper!"

"I won't!" Joel ran out the door and to the kitchen. As he walked inside he smelled the wonderful scent of pork, mashed potatoes and apple pie! He reached for a stray slice of an apple lying on the table.

"What ah you's doin' in my kitchen?!"

Joel jumped and threw the slice down. "I was just- I thought- ummm-"

"You *neva* come n' take food from dis here kitchen, witout askin' da cook! And, dat's *me*!"

"Yes, ma'am." It was only now that Joel realized that he was speaking to an elderly slave woman. She let out a large sigh.

"You mus' be Joe Harris, Snelson's new boy." she said.

"Yes, ma'am. I am" he said proudly, trying to hide the fact that he didn't like being called "Snelson's boy".

"I'm real sorry, ma'am. I was just hungry." he said.

"Well, I s'pose dats okay *dis* time. You's didn't know da rules. Go on! Eat dis!" she said handing him a whole apple.

"Oh, thank you!" he took a big bite out of the side.

"I's Aunt Crissy. I do all da cookin' an weavin'"

"Nice ta meet ya!" Joel said with his mouth full.

"You's worse dan my Harbert!" she said hitting him in the leg with her cane.

Crissy was not a tall woman, or very slender. But, what she lacked in stature, she made up for in arm strength.

Joel dropped the apple and leaned over to rub his aching leg.

Aunt Crissy suddenly burst out laughing.

"Yessah, Harbert's gonna like you! Follow me!"

Joel was confused. But he followed, anyway. She led him through a side door in the kitchen and under a covered passageway that was about four feet long, then up two steps and into a little cabin. The cabin had two little rooms. One had a bed, a wooden rocking chair and a stone fireplace and another had a big weaving loom, a little stool and a second fireplace.

In the first room sat an old man in the rocking chair carving what looked like a toy wagon. On the floor sat four wide-eyed children eagerly listening to the old man's gentle words. On the bed sat a small boy, no more then two, playing with a wooden rabbit.

"Ol' Harbert! Sorry to in-a-rupt your stary time, but you's got ta meet Snelson's new boy!"

Joel wanted to ask her to at least call him Snelson's

apprentice, but he decided he'd better not.

"Dis here is Joe Harris!"

"Ah! Joe Harris! Marster Turner spoke mighty fine o' you boy!"

"Joe, I want you ter meet Marster Turner's chilllins" Aunt Crissy said, gesturing toward the children on the floor of the cabin.

"Dis here is Wattie, Willie, Lucy and Michael. And over dar on da bed is little Marster Joey. He's da baby." She patted Joey lovingly on the shoulder. Joel smiled and waved to the small herd of kids staring back at him.

" Well, Marse Joe, I'ze was 'bout ta tell da chillins a stary. You wanna jawn us?" Ol' Harbert asked.

"What type of story?" Joel asked.

"Well, its called Brer Rabbit and the Briar Patch" Old Harbert said matter-of-factly.

"Old Harbert's always tellin' stories 'bout Brer Rabbit!" said Wattie.

"Jus as my Grandaddy tole me when I was a youngin!" Old Harbert said.

Settling In

"Okay! I guess I can stay for a bit!" Joel took a seat on the floor in front of the fire and listened as Old Harbert began to tell about Brer Rabbit, Brer Fox, Brer Bear and all of their adventures. Joel was in awe of the magical lore unfolding before him.

He would come back to listen day after day and night after night during his years at Turnwold.

Hours passed and soon Joel and the other children went to eat dinner in the big house.

Dinner was good and Joel enjoyed meeting the mistress of the house, Mrs. Louisa. And he was excited to talk with Wattie and William some more. Despite the fact that William was about half his age, they seemed to click.

After supper, Joel was sent to his new room in the "ell." He walked in to find a wardrobe, a bed with a side table and a little desk. Uncle George had already brought his grandmother's trunk in and set it on the bed.

He quietly unpacked his belongings and filled the drawers of the little wardrobe. He looked out the window at the dusk settling over the plantation and before he could help himself, he climbed out.

He ran past the kitchen and the little periwinkle covered graveyard until he found the perfect tree situated on a little mound of earth. He plopped down, leaned against it and silently watched as the sun set over Turnwold Plantation.

He was all alone. His mother was at home in Eatonton. Mr. Turner had long since retired to his room, and the slaves were all asleep after a hard day's work. He was all alone, but he wasn't lonely. For Joel, sitting alone was one of the greatest blessings Turnwold had to offer. Unlike in the bustling town of Eatonton, he could always find a quiet place to sit and read or think. *Turnwold offers the perfect amount of loneliness,* Joel thought to himself. Lonely enough to make him think about life in ways it might not otherwise occur to him to think about. It brought him face to face with himself. But, not lonely enough to put him in low spirits.

He sat there for hours and watched as the stars filled the sky. Eventually, he headed back to his little room in the ell and went to sleep.

Chapter Eight

A NEW DISCOVERY

The next day, Joel woke bright and early and headed to the printing shop. He walked in to find Mr. Snelson working the heavy Washington #2 with the aid of an older, slave boy. Joel slowly took a step into the room.

"Ah! There ye are, boy! I was worried I scared ye off after yesterday." Mr. Snelson's thick Irish accent echoed loudly through the little building.

"Did you have me replaced, sir?" Joel asked, his voice quivering.

"No! No! Floyd is just here to help me lift the press!" Mr Snelson put a hand on Floyd's shoulder and signaled for him to leave.

"Come, my boy." He waved for Joel to come to the corner of the room. Joel obeyed and was surprised when a dirty, oversized apron landed on his shoulders.

"Ay" he said with a sigh. "It's a wee bit large for ye, but I s'pose you'll grow into it!"

Mr. Snelson took a step back to see Joel in his new uniform.

"For now, you'll sweep the floor and do whatever else I tell ye. Ye may practice to lay type when y'aren't busy, and soon I'll let ye do that full time."

"Thank you, sir!" Joel tied the apron behind his back and picked up the broom to begin sweeping.

"Well, that's that! Let's get started! We have a busy day ahead of us! 'Come what come may, time and the hour runs through the roughest day!' " Mr. Snelson said with a little jump.

"*Macbeth*!" Joel said in surprise.

"Ye know Shakespeare?"

"Yes! My mama and I read it all the time!"

" 'There is nothing either good or bad, but thinking makes it so.' " Mr. Snelson was testing him now.

"*Hamlet*!" Joel said proudly.

"Aye. But do you know this one? 'If you prick us, do we not bleed? If you tickle us, do we not laugh? If you poison us, do we not die? And if you wrong us, shall we not revenge?' "

A New Discovery

Joel was perplexed. He had never heard this one! He thought and thought but still, nothing came to mind.

"Ah! I got ye!" Mr. Snelson said giddily.

"What is it?" Joel asked eagerly.

"*The Merchant of Venice.* Looks like ye need to get yourself a copy!"

"I don't understand. I read every Shakespeare play in the whole library! How did I miss one?"

"The library in Eatonton?" Mr. Snelson asked.

"Yes, sir. That's the only library within miles of here!"

"Wrong."

"What?"

"That's the only *public* library within miles of here. It has near five hundred books in it. But I know of a bigger one!"

"Really? Where?" Joel stopped sweeping and looked at Mr. Snelson who smiled slyly.

"Across the house from your bedroom."

Joel was really confused"What do you mean?"

"I mean, it's across the house from your bedroom! In the other ell!"

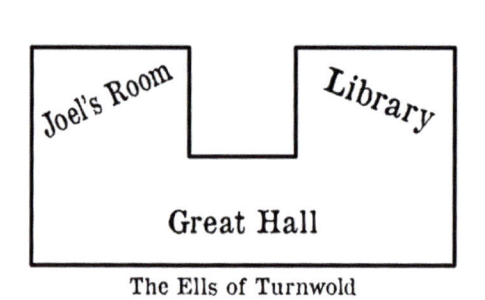

"Mr. Turner has a library? In the house?" Joel asked excitedly.

"Aye. Five thousand volumes, all in one place! Joseph has something to be proud of, for sure!"

"Can I see it? Please!?" Joel was overwhelmed. He had to see this library!

"Well, Mr. Turner said I was not to let you in his study unless on business. And, the library *is* his study. So, you'd better not."

"Oh. Alright" Disappointed, Joel continued to sweep the floor behind the stove.

🐇🐇🐇

The day went on. Mr. Snelson laid the type, Floyd worked the press and Joel swept the floor, wiped up ink spills, kept the stove burning and ran errands.

A New Discovery

By two o'clock, the next week's edition of *The Countryman* was complete and ready to be proofread by Mr. Turner.

Joel watched as Mr. Snelson carefully picked up the wet, freshly printed newspaper. Awkwardly holding the paper by the corners with the thumb and index finger of both hands, he walked in a slouched, half waddle over to the door of the office.

Joel ran over and held the door open for him.

"What are ye doin' me-boy?" Mr. Snelson asked.

"Um, I was getting the door for you, sir!"

"Come here, lad!" With a jerk of his head, he gestured for Joel to come over to him. As Joel walked closer, Mr. Snelson extended both of his arms offering the paper to Joel.

"You want *me* to deliver the paper, sir?" Joel asked.

"Aye. Joesph will be waiting in his library to edit the paper."

"The *library?!*"

"Go, lad! You know where it is! The paper should be dry by the time you reach the house. Don't forget to tell Terrell what ye are doin'!"

"I'll remember!"

Joel ran to the big house and pushed the doors open. He started running to the ell where the library was when he ran straight into Uncle George.

"And what do you's think you's er doin', Marse Joe?" he asked with a stern look on his face.

"I am just delivering the first draft of next week's paper to Mr. Turner!"

"Alrighty, Marse Joe, but slow down! You er goin' farster den Brer Rabbit in huntin' season!"

"Will do, Uncle George!" Joel walked as fast as he could to the big double doors of the library.

"Marse Joe!" Uncle George called. "Let me go in first! It proper fo' da butler to introduce visitors to da marsters office."

"Okay...sorry" Joel said, a little embarrassed at his excitement.

Uncle George opened the door and stuck his head in.

"'S'cuse me, sir. Marse Joe is here ta see you, sir. He has

da draft of da *Countryman* for you's ta see."

"Let him in, please, Mr. Terrell." Mr. Turner said.

Uncle George turned to Joel who was standing outside the door.

"Don't be long, now! Mr. Turner's got a mighty lot of things he must get done!"

"I'll hurry!" Joel stepped into the big, beautiful room. The walls were lined with book shelves stretching all the way up to the ceiling. Tall ladders on rollers were scattered around the shelves. Mr. Turner's big desk sat in the middle of the room with couches and chairs surrounding it. Joel had never seen so many books in one place! It was beautiful! He stepped toward the first case. He looked up at all the dusty, leather-bound books. He was tempted to grab one, but he held himself back.

"Joel."

He jumped and nearly dropped the paper. He had completely forgotten his original purpose for coming!

"Do you have the draft for me?" Mr. Turner asked.

"Oh! Yes, sir! I do!" He skidded over to Mr. Turner's desk and laid the paper down in front of him.

"Here you are, sir! Freshly printed for your readin' enjoyment!"

Mr. Turner looked at Joel curiously out of the corner of his eye and quickly put his hands in the air.

"Oh! Uh, not that fresh, sir! It's dry, alright!"

"Thank you, Joel! You may go now." He set his glasses on the tip of his nose and picked up the paper.

Joel sighed. He just wanted to stay a little longer and look at the books! He started to walk out of the room when he saw it: a set of encyclopedias! He had never seen one in real life! Encyclopedia sets were huge and very expensive.

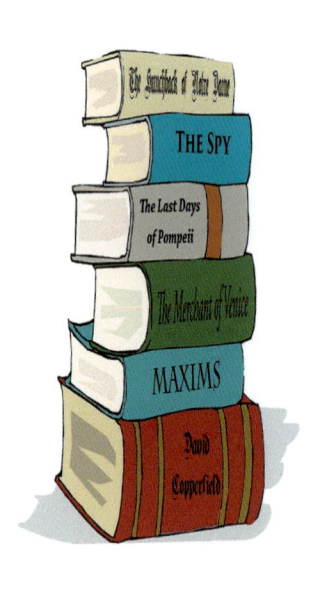

He found himself running his fingers over the tops of all the books. One after another, all part of the same encyclopedia!

Then he looked up and saw a Brother's Grimm collection and *The Hunchback of Notre Dame*! He saw a book about the last days of Pompeii, and another called *The Spy*. He was intrigued. He wanted to read every book on these shelves.

"I see you like my library."

Joel spun around. How long had he been standing there?

"Oh, yes, sir! I love to read!" Joel said shyly.

"Well, my home is your home now, and if you ever want to borrow a book, just ask!" He moved down the wall of books and grabbed one off the top shelf.

"How about *David Copperfield*? It may be a little difficult for you to read but it is a classic, and I believe you might find it enjoyable!"

"Oh, well, you see, I've already read that one, sir. And I did find it quite enjoyable!"

"Really?"

"Yes, sir! I was wondering if I could borrow *The Merchant of Venice*? I am trying to read all of Shakespeare's plays, and I haven't read that one, yet!"

"Well, of course! If that's what you want!" He grabbed the big book and handed it to Joel.

"Thank you, sir! I'll start reading this now!"

"You have to get back to work first!" Mr. Turner said with

a chuckle.

"Oh, yes! Thank you, Mr. Turner!" He started heading for the door.

"Wait, Joel!"

Joel whipped around.

Mr. Turner grabbed a book from his desk.

"I would like you to select fillers for the paper from this book: La Rochefoucauld's *Maxims*. I believe you will find it fascinating."

"I'm honored, sir!" As Joel took the book from Mr. Turner he couldn't help but think the man must be some sort of miscellaneous genius.

Chapter Nine

A BIG STEP

Days turned into weeks, and weeks into months. Joel spent his days in the printing office with Mr. Snelson, or under a tree somewhere eating an apple and picking fillers for *The Countryman* from *Maxims*, *Anecdotes* and *Lacon*.

He spent his nights in the slave quarters, listening to stories, and just enjoying himself with his 'family' of the one-hundred and twenty slaves on Turnwold.

His whole life Joel had been mocked by the kids at school for his bright red hair and freckles, but in the quarters, the slaves taught him that looking different wasn't a bad thing.

He felt more at home with the slaves than in the big house with the Turners. And, he ended up taking most of his suppers with them, around a big campfire where they roasted potatoes, told stories and sang songs – some happy, some sad, but all beautiful.

The Road to the Briar Patch

He spent the most time of all with Old Harbert, Aunt Betsy and Uncle George. They told the best stories, and they treated him like a son. Joel couldn't be happier! He enjoyed his days in the printing office with Mr. Snelson setting type for the paper, quoting Shakespeare and even working the press some!

Mr. Turner ensured that Joel was not missing out on an education by not going to school. He suggested books to read that would be beneficial to him in the future, and made sure to make lessons out of daily life as much as he could.

With all he was learning from the slaves, Mr. Snelson and Mr. Turner, Joel thought he was getting more out of not going to school than had he gone.

Turnwold, with its forests, big houses, slave quarters and printing office, as well as the fictional world of Chickapenn Hill where Brer Rabbit lived- that was Joel's classroom.

As the years went by Joel began to develop a talent for writing. Every once in a while, he would write a poem or a short story and give it to Mr. Turner with the week's other submissions to the paper, but he would sign it with a made-up name, like Sam Jones or Bucky White.

A Big Step

Most of the time Mr. Turner would decline the little articles but sometimes he would include them in the week's paper.

The year was 1864. It had been two years since he had made his move to Turnwold, and Joel was ready to make another big change. He was going to sign one of his articles with his own name and submit it to the paper.

He carefully picked his favorite article that he had written in the recent weeks and edited it to ensure that it was some of his best work. Slowly, he picked up his pen and signed:

Joel C Harris

He folded it up and put it in an extra envelope from the

printing office. He stacked it with the rest of the submissions that Mr. Snelson had received that week and headed off for Mr. Turner's office.

He walked up to the big door with Uncle George at his side. Uncle George opened the door and stuck his head in.

"Marse Joe is here to da'liva da week's submissions, sir."

"Ah! Send him in!" Mr. Turner said.

Joel walked slowly into the room, trying to hide his nervousness.

"Here you go, sir!" Joel said sheepishly.

"Is everything alright, Joel?"

"Yes, sir! I- I'm just in a hurry to get back to Mr. Snelson...."

"Well, alright. You run along, then!" Joel was gone before you could say 'rabbit'.

🐰🐰🐰

When Joel arrived back at the printing office, he grabbed his oversized apron off the wall and headed over to his post at the desk where he was to lay type.

A Big Step

"How did it go, lad? Did Mr. Turner like yer column?" Mr. Snelson asked, as he appeared from behind the stove.

"I didn't tell him. I just handed it to him with the other submissions, as usual, and left" Joel said as he examined an oddly shaped 'L' stamp. "Do you think he's read it, yet?"

"Patience, me boy! 'How poor are they that have not patience!'" Mr. Snelson replied.

"Okay." Joel said, exasperated.

"You forgot something."

"Oh! *Othello*!"

"Right you are, lad!"

Joel worked hard in an attempt to distract himself from the agony of waiting for a reply. Mr. Turner had rejected his articles before, but the benefit of using a pen name was that he didn't have to face the criticism. He would just try harder next time.

He feared what Mr. Turner might say. What if he finds it horrible and decides to oust him? He couldn't think straight. He needed to calm down.

But Mr. Turner didn't send out rejection letters until Thursday! It could be days before he heard anything!

He took a deep breath and then, continued the long, tedious job of laying the type for the newspaper, one letter at a time, backwards. He had learned to spell backwards so well, that he would occasionally start writing a letter to his mother backwards and have to start over! Cautiously, he set out the words:

Three time beaver hats for sale - the last of the season.

He looked at it, pleased. He then grabbed the roller and applied ink to the stamps. He put a paper down on the table and carefully flipped the wet stamps on to it. He hammered the stamp case with a little mallet, and then lifted the stamps to reveal the finished ad.

A Big Step

Three fine beaver hats for sale - the last of the season.

He wasn't completely sure if he spelled "beaver" right, so he took it to Mr. Snelson for inspection before including the advertisement in the full paper.

🐇 🐇 🐇

He continued to distract himself for days, and still no reply came. He was more anxious than ever.

Mr. Snelson tried to calm him down with quotations from Shakespeare, but he would not be consoled.

🐇 🐇 🐇

One pastime that kept Joel's hands and head busy and his pockets full was rabbit hunting in his spare time. Joel would often make three to four kills an afternoon. These rabbits were quickly sold for 20 cents apiece in town. It was a paying job that insured that one day, when Joel left

Turnwold he'd have some money to start his new life.

Thursday rolled around and he still hadn't heard anything. But he knew what had to be done. He had to go to Mr. Turners office to pick up the rejection letters, and he couldn't pretend that he hadn't submitted a column.

Confidently, he walked into Mr. Turner's office and over to the desk.

"I was wondering when you would get here" Mr. Turner said, not taking his eyes off his work.

"I'm sorry, sir! I didn't think I was late."

"Oh, you're not. The letters are on that table over there, next to the door."

"Um, thank you sir. I will have these delivered."

"Thank you, Joel."

Joel started walking to the door, confused.

"See ya later, Mr. Turner!"

"Oh, Joel!"

Joel spun around.

"Yes sir?"

A Big Step

"Don't you want to know what I thought of your article?" Mr. Turner said, looking up from the newspaper he was studying.

"Oh. Yes, sir! I do!"

"Come take a seat, son."

Joel walked over and plopped down in a big, red cushioned chair in front of Mr. Turner's desk. In the soft, velvet chair he felt more like a formal business partner, coming to discuss important business with the prominent plantation owner and newspaper editor, than the crude, inexperienced Printer's Devil that he was.

He straightened his back and tried to look as dignified as he felt sitting in that fancy chair. He took a deep breath in, trying to hide his tension.

"I regret to inform you, that I must deny your article" Mr. Turner said in a sorrowful tone. "I hate to turn down your first article, but it's just not up to the standards of *The Countryman*." Joel was shocked, but not that his article didn't make it. He half expected that. He was surprised that Mr. Turner just came out and said it that way! His eyes drifted downward as he tried to hide his disappointment.

Sensing his disappointment, Mr. Turner stood up, walked around the desk and sat down in the chair next to Joel. He set a gentle hand on Joel's knee.

"I admit, it does have merit. I can see that your natural talent for writing far exceeds most children your age. But it had some problems. Problems that I wish to help you with. How would you like me to teach you the ethics of good writing?"

"I- I would love that, sir!" Joel's whole demeanor changed in an instant.

"But for now, I will give you this bit of advise: In writing from now on, first select a good, worthy subject. Second, stick to that subject. And, third, say what you have to say in as few words as possible."

"But sir, I-"

"All this is for your good" Mr. Turner interrupted.

"Yes, sir. Thank you!"

"You're welcome, Joel."

The rejection only encouraged Joel to keep trying.

Mr. Turner helped Joel cultivate his talents until he produced something worthy of the paper.

A Big Step

Joel wrote many poems and articles for *The Countryman* after that. He kept the advise that Mr. Turner had given him that day close to his heart, and always followed his "three rules of writing."

Chapter Ten

A CELEBRATION

One night, after a special dinner with the Turner family celebrating the release of his newest and most impressive poem, "Nelly White," Joel sat on his bed packing a small sack.

He rummaged through the drawer of his bedside table and found a pen and a single piece of paper. It wasn't enough for what he was going to do, but paper was in short supply.

He slid off his mattress, taking his quilt with him, and reached under his bed. He felt around on the rough, wooden floor, desperately trying to avoid the big, nasty cockroaches, until he found his stash of old editions of *The Countryman* that Mr. Snelson had let him keep. He stood up and counted the papers. He had six full newspapers. That seemed good. He stuffed them in his sack with the pen and threw it over his shoulder.

A Celebration

Joel quietly pushed the bedroom door open, just slightly, to see if anyone was still up and out of their rooms.

The Turners tended to go to bed really early. Joel thought it must be because Mr. Turner always woke up early to start his day at four or five in the morning. He could hear Mrs. Turner playing the piano in the parlor, so he shut the door and retreated back to his room and looked around for another means of escape.

Then, he remembered the window. He hadn't climbed out the window since his first day at Turnwold almost three years ago.

Joel tiptoed over to the window and tried to pull it open with all his might. After a considerable bit of pulling it popped open and he lunged back in surprise, landing on his bed. Dazed, he sat up and examined his accomplishment. He smiled, grabbed his bag and leaped out, careful to avoid the Black-Eyed Susans that Mrs. Turner had planted under his room last spring.

It was dark now, but he could see the flickering light of

the bonfire at the Quarters, way off in the distance. He paused to look at the beautiful light amongst the little cabins and trees, across a long field of neatly cut grass.

Until that moment he hadn't really thought about how much he loved it here. After a brief intermission to marvel over the plantation, he started to run around the house.

It was so dark, that he couldn't see past his knees. He knew he had a better chance of getting to the Quarters without getting lost *(again)* if he started from the front of the house where a dirt path marked the way. He could use the path to feel his way, until the light from the bonfire illuminated the ground.

He arrived at the front of the house where two gas lamps lit up the yard. He snuck around the yard until he found the path, and started on his way.

About half way to the Quarters, he began to hear rustling in the bushes. He slowed down and tried to quiet his steps. A tree next to the path suddenly shook.

He jumped, as a pine cone rolled out in front of him. And, then another. And, another!

He cautiously stepped around the pine cones, trying not

A Celebration

to make a sound. He didn't have a lantern, so if a bear or some other wild animal was hiding in the trees it would track him by sound.

He stopped suddenly as a pine cone crushed beneath his foot on the pitch-black ground. He held his breath, and tried to keep completely still. He heard whatever was in the trees start to move, slowly, on all fours, right towards him!

Then, it lunged out of the forest and started bounding to him!

He dropped his sack and ran. He didn't look back. He was right outside the Quarters now. He turned around to see what had been pursuing him.

The creature had not moved at all. Then it stood up on its hind legs and started walking up the path.

Confused, he walked ever so slowly, towards the creature. As his confidence grew, he started to walk faster, and faster, until he was running.

The dark creature at the other end of the path started running as well. Before he could do anything about it, he was running, face first, into the creature that had just tried to attack him. They hit each other hard and both bounced back onto the dirt.

"Ouch!" said the creature.

"What are ya doing?" shouted Joel.

"You dropped your bag!"

"Willie?" said Joel recognizing the voice of Mr. Turner's oldest son. "I thought you were in bed!"

"Nope. I've been out here with Wattie." Willie responded.

"Where is she?" Joel asked. He knew that when the Turner kids were outside, it was Wattie's job to babysit them. Willie was only nine, and was never suppose to be alone. Especially at night.

"Aw, we was already goin' to see Uncle George when you came. I 'sided to scare ya! So Wattie went on ahead." Willie was bouncing all over the place.

"You sure did scare me!'

"Good!" Willie said with a jump.

"We better go catch up with Wattie."

"Let's go!" Willie started running down the path towards the light of the fire, and Joel followed behind.

A Celebration

As they arrived at the Quarters they made their way through the maze of cabins, until they came upon a group of people sitting on logs around the big bonfire.

They saw Wattie sitting on the grass, her knees pulled to her chest, looking up at Uncle George with sincere admiration as he passionately spun his tale.

Willie ran over and plopped down next to her on the ground.

Uncle George paused his story to turn to greet him and pat him on shoulder.

Joel was about to go and join them when he saw Aunt Crissy on the other side of the crowded bonfire. He walked around the tall, warm flames over to where she was standing roasting something over the fire with a long stick.

"Joe! You's here! We'z thought you was comin'!" Aunt Crissy said gleefully. She leaned over and hugged him with her free arm.

"Hi, Aunt Crissy!"

Aunt Crissy pulled her stick out of the fire to reveal roasted potatoes.

Joel's mouth watered at the sight of the salted potato

goodness.

"I'z left da skin on just fo' you, hon!"

"Oh, thank ya! You're the best!" Joel shouted with glee.

"Jus' wait a bit darlin', they'z hot!" Aunt Crissy laid the potatoes on a kitchen rag to cool.

"How was supper in da big house?" she asked.

"It was wonderful! I particularly liked the pie! Maybe you could make an extra one next time and we can eat it here!"

"Thank you'z, Joe, I will. But I meant the part 'bout your poem."

"Oh, yeah! It was great! Mr. Turner said that he's gotten letters from people sayin' how much they liked the poem and look forward to more!"

Aunt Crissy smiled and shook her head in unbrideled happiness for this young man that she had watched bloom. She wiped her hands on her apron and then, putting her hand behind Joel's back, led him to a log and gestured to sit down.

"Joe," she said, looking him square in the face "I'z is so proud of you!" She leaned over and gave him another suffocating hug. "One of these days, boy, you'z gonna be in high cotton!"

Joel smiled. He always felt a little uncomfortable when people flattered his work, but he loved Aunt Crissy and he knew Aunt Crissy loved him, so he let himself enjoy it for once.

Aunt Crissy sat up straight and smoothed the wrinkles in her apron, a tear in her eye. She looked at Joel and smiled.

"Tomorrow can you'z read me that new poem?" Aunt Crissy asked.

"'Course! I'd love to!" Joel said excitedly. He enjoyed his time sitting by the fire in Aunt Crissy and Old Harbert's cabin reading them the newspaper, or something he was working on.

"I might even come over before breakfast!" Joel said with a beam.

"I'z sure we'd love that!" Aunt Crissy chuckled. Now, go'z get your potato sticks!"

Joel jumped up and went to the little table Aunt Crissy had been working at, next to the the bonfire. He tapped the stick with the tip of his finger to make sure it wasn't too hot, and then stuffed half of it into his mouth without hesitation.

The Road to the Briar Patch

"What you doin' boy!?" shouted Uncle George from across the sea of people eating and chatting around the fire. "You gonna choke you'zelf!"

Joel walked over to Uncle George. Wattie and Willie giggled at his puffed out squirrel cheeks. Joel swallowed hard and tried to hide his embarrassment. He sat down on the log next to Uncle George with the rest of his potato stick.

"Can you finish the story now?" asked Willie.

"Course, suga'!"

Joel pulled his pen and leftover newspapers out of his bag. As Uncle George told his story, Joel made notes on the back of his newspaper. He wanted to always remember the way the story would magically unfold as Uncle George told it in his enchanting way.

"Now this here tale didn't just happen yesterday, nor the day before. No! It was a long time ago. The critters: they was closer to the folks. And the folk: they was closer to the critters. And if you'll 'scuse me for saying so, it was better all around."

The night went on and Joel sat by the fire with his family of slaves, listening to stories, eating delicious food and

A Celebration

talking to the 'Aunts and Uncles' that he loved. This was his happy place.

As the evening ended and he hurried back to his room there was a zip in his step and a song in his heart.

Epilogue

MAY 9, 1865

"Who's there!?" Seventeen year old Joel sat up in bed with a start. He was sure he heard something, but now all he could hear was the distant sound of roosters crowing. He let himself relax and slumped back on his pillow. But as soon as his head hit the bed again, he roused and realized it was morning and he needed to get to work.

He jumped out of bed, pulled on his trousers and his vest and quickly tied up his leather boots, then bounded out his bedroom door. He walked though the quiet, early morning halls of the great house and couldn't help but wonder where everyone was.

Uncle George was nowhere to be seen and he was usually the first one to be lurking around in the morning.

With his curiosity and concern growing Joel began to peer into the rooms as he passed them, looking for any signs of life. He saw the door to Mrs. Louisa's sitting room

Epilogue

propped open and against his better judgment he stuck his head in.

"Ada?" he whispered, calling for Mrs. Louisa's servant. No reply came. No Uncle George and no Ada? This was strange. He thought he must have the time wrong. The sun was still low in the sky, so it could be earlier than he'd first thought.

He decided to just go to the printing office and see about Mr. Snelson. He slowly opened the tall, heavy front door and slowly pulled it closed, trying to be as quiet as possible so he didn't wake the Turners.

He walked down the dirt path that had been worn from four years of Joel going back and forth from the printing office.

Suddenly, he heard a commotion on the main road about thirty feet away. He ran over to the edge of the driveway and his mouth dropped open when he saw the source of the noise. There were four big carts being pulled by tall, muscular war horses. About a dozen men walked alongside, guiding them. The men were all wearing blue coats. They were *Union soldiers!* Joel stood paralyzed with fear. *What was going on?*

"Hey, Elmer! Look at Lil' Pink-head over here!" one of the men shouted.

"Oh! What do we have here?" said a second man.

"Oi' laddy!" He turned to the first man in a mocking way. "Do ye want to go leprechaun huntin' with me?" The two men doubled over in laughter. They stumbled around saying things about their "pots of gold" and "four leaf clovers" and "freckle cream."

At this point Joel could tell they were talking about him so he darted behind the nearest fence. It didn't offer much protection from the rude soldiers' stares, but Joel was paralyzed in the moment and didn't even think to run away.

As soon as they passed out of sight, Joel bounced up and ran as fast as he could, not even stopping at the printing office until he reached the Quarters. It was desolate. The embers on the usual morning bonfire were dim and fading. He walked between the cabins, dodging the chickens and goats running wild out of their pens. He walked up the stairs of the nearest cabin and stuck his head in the door. It was empty. The cots had been stripped of their blankets and the pans were no longer hanging on the wall. And, all that was left of the fire wood were a few loose splinters. As he stepped around the empty cabin he felt something soft under his feet. He knelt down and found that he had stepped on a small rag doll. He picked it up, held it in his hands and looked into its small, blank face. *How could they do something like this?* he wondered, blaming the Union Soldiers for kidnapping everyone and looting their homes.

He walked back to the printing office with the rag doll hanging out of his back pocket. He pulled the door open to find no sign of Mr. Snelson. *Had they taken him, too? If so, why did the soldiers let Joel off so easily?*

He ran back to the big house, stopping to hide whenever he heard a noise he thought might be more carts. As he neared the house, he saw smoke coming from the kitchen chimney. He felt a rush of relief and ran with new-found speed to the out-building. He burst through the door to find Aunt Crissy kneading dough.

"Joe Harris!" She said stopping her task and running to embrace him. "Where you been? George has been lookin' hither and tither for ya!"

"What's going on?" Joel asked, trying to break away from

her tight bear hug. "Where is everybody?"

Seeing his concern, Aunt Crissy sighed. Her face looked grave.

"Maybe Marster Turner ought to be the one to tell you."

"Tell me what?" Joel could feel his heart beating in his throat. *What had those Yankees done to everybody!?*

"He's in his study." Aunt Crissy said solemnly.

Joel turned around and walked back to the front door of the big house. He had just begun to pull the heavy, brass handle when the door came open on its own. Uncle George stepped out from behind it and nodded politely to Joel.

"I'z knew you'd come back her' sometime or other" he said with a wink.

"I need to see Mr. Turner." Joel responded.

"I'ze also knew you would wanna do dat" Uncle George said with a familiar twinkle in his eye. He led Joel to the back of the big house. As they passed through the halls, Joel heard crying from Mrs. Louisa's sitting room. She sounded really distressed. He could hear Wattie trying to console her, but apparently failing. As they passed the parlor he heard all sorts of commotion, but the door was shut so he couldn't see

Epilogue

who was inside.

Uncle George pushed open the door to Mr. Turner's study, stuck his head in and said something that Joel couldn't make out. He pulled out and turned towards Joel.

"He'll see'z ya now Marse Joe." Uncle George gave Joel's hand a reassuring squeeze and then nudged him into the office.

Mr. Turner was sitting at his desk, his head in his hands, muttering to himself. The unusually dim lighting gave the room a somber, eerie sense that made Joel feel uneasy. He walked apprehensively over and sat in the big, comfy chair across from Mr. Turner.

"Mr. Turner-" Joel began, but was cut off.

"As an editor, Joel, I am supposed to be a bold lion. But right know I feel like a mere street rat. I'm losing everything, Joel. They are stripping me of everything I've built as if it's their right to do so."

"Who is 'they,' sir?" Joel asked, his hands shaking.

"General Lee's army has been captured." Mr. Turner stared at Joel with wet eyes. This normally strong man looked more pitiful than Joel had ever seen him. "And, the balance of our armies, through their generals, are negotiating an abomination of our flag and our country."

He paused to let it sink in. Joel's mind was whirling. He had never been much for politics or war. In fact he tried to avoid them when he could, but this was big. Really, big. He had no idea how it might affect him. He just sat in silence and awaited the next blow.

"As a result, all of the slaves are free. A few have chosen to leave and seek new lives. A large majority, in particular the older slaves and their families, have chosen to remain here.

"I've offered to continue to feed them as well as supply wages if they choose to stay." Joel looked over his shoulder to see Uncle George listening in through the crack in the door. *He must have chosen to stay,* he thought.

"And, as for *The Countryman,* I feel that if I can't edit my *own* paper as freeman, I will not edit it at all. I will drop the paper back to only quarterly editions for now, but I have chosen to no longer make any mentions to political affairs. Not even in comics. The Yankee's will have new laws regarding how much a paper may say about such affairs and I feel if I cannot speak my mind and state my opinion on a

Epilogue

topic, I would rather not speak of it. Period. Do you understand?"

"Yes sir. But what about me? Can I stay?"

"My boy, you can stay as long as you wish. But I must implore you to explore other employment options. I can only imagine that in this new era, a paper of my standing won't last long. But you are always welcome in my house, Joel Harris."

Joel managed a weak smile as he turned toward the door to leave. Uncle George put a familiar arm around Joel's shoulders and walked him toward the parlor where the sound of talking was getting louder. Uncle George opened the door and inside stood Mr. Snelson, Aunt Crissy, Ada and even Old Harbert had managed to carefully make his way into the big house with his cane to gather with the others on this monumental day. The room was crowded with the now former slaves milling about discussing their plans to stay on the Turner's plantation in this new era. Wattie, Willie, Lucy, Michael and little Joey were now in the room, too, going from person to person looking up at them for reassurance.

As Joel looked around the beautiful room he thought of

his own mother, at home 9 miles away. This life hadn't seen fit to give him a father. But, he thought, he had found several unlikely substitute fathers: Uncle George had watched over him in a fatherly way since his first day on the plantation, doing his best to help Joel stay out of trouble. Mr. Snelson had taken him under his wing to teach him his trade of printing, just like he'd do for a son, all the while quizzing him on his Shakespeare. Mr. Turner had taken him in and helped give him his voice as he tested out his writing for the first time. And, dear Old Harbert, who was so faithful to always tell him the stories of Brer Rabbit and the other forest friends that encouraged him to find his own "Laffin' Place" and ignore any Brer Foxes that may come along. Yes, he had many fathers who had all prepared him well for whatever lay ahead.

Very soon, circumstances were such that Joel was forced to leave Turnwold. He went to his little room in the left "ell" and peered under the bed that he'd slept in for more than

Epilogue

four years. He pulled out his little tin box of Rabbit money and opened it up, ready to start his new life with his savings he'd so carefully put away. However, when he examined the contents, he realized that he'd been paid solely with Confederate coins. He was broke. *What would Brer Rabbit, do?* he thought. With a quickening heartbeat, he jumped up, more determined than ever to make a brand new start.

Deeper in the Briar Patch

QUESTIONS AND ANSWERS FOR CURIOUS MINDS

HOW DID JOEL GET HIS NAME?

Mary Harris, Joel's mother, was well-loved and as a single mother, received help from many people, including Dr. Henry Branham, husband of her aunt, Verlinda Harris. Dr. Branham was present at Joel's birth, along with his brother who was also training to become a doctor. His brother's name was Joel.

WHAT IS A LIVERY?

A livery is a type of uniform worn by butlers in a big house. BUT, a livery stable is a stable where horses are kept for hire.

WHAT IS A WHITE MUD GULLEY?

White mud is another name for Georgia kaolinite, a white clay that is in abundance in parts of Georgia. A gulley is a trench washed out by rain water.

What is a Printer's Devil?

A Printer's Devil is just the name of an apprentice in a printing establishment who performs tasks such as mixing ink and getting type. There are several stories that claim to tell the reason that they are called "devils." One possible reason is that the apprentices were often required to take the used type to the "hellbox" where they would either be sorted or melted down in a fire and recast.

Did you know the phrase "Mind your Ps and Qs" came from the old print shops?

The Printer's Devils had to be very careful to lay their Ps and Qs correctly because a P would look like a Q when it was laid backwards to print.

The Road to the Briar Patch

Who was Andrew Jackson Downing?

Mr. Downing was the prominent American landscape designer who was called upon to help design the gardens and forests at Turnwold. He, along with a partner, designed the grounds at the White House and the Smithsonian Castle in Washington DC.

What were Maxims, Anecdotes and Lacon?

The Countryman was not a newspaper in the same sense of the word we use today. As a small Plantation paper (most likely the only one in the U.S.), it was mostly a literary journal with book reviews, essays, short stories and opinion articles. Rochefoucauld's *Maxims*, Percy's *Anecdotes* and Colton's *Lacon* were all books that were full of short sayings that made wonderful paper fillers when *The Countryman* had a little space to fill.

Deeper in the Briar Patch

Joel Chandler Harris

Further Reading and Discovery

- *The Life and Letters of Joel Chandler Harris* by Julia Collier Harris
- *Joel Chandler Harris and His Home; a Sketch* by Myrta Lockett Avary
- *Uncle Remus, His Songs and Sayings* by Joel Chandler Harris
- *On the Plantation* by Joel Chandler Harris
- www.wrensnest.org
- www.pencilsandpixiedust.com
- Walt Disney's "Song of the South"
- "Walt Disney's Wonderful World of Color: A Tribute to Joel Chandler Harris" television special

About the Author

Chloe Shelton is a 16 year old homechooled student and self-proclaimed Nerd Princess who loves all things Disney, Super Heroes and Tolkien.

As a student of filmmaking she premiered her first feature-length film at just barely 14 years old. She's worked on professional film sets around her hometown and has been involved as an apprentice in film and film-editing since the age of 11.
The Road to the Briar Patch is her first novel.

In her spare time, Chloe is the head Mouseketeer at her website, PencilsAndPixieDust.com, where she features in-depth, fun looks at rides and attractions in Walt Disney World as well as audio adventures that she writes, records and edits.

Chloe's love for bringing stories to life is what propels her writing, whether in books, movies or audio adventures.

PICKLES & POPCORN
PRODUCTIONS

Printed in Poland
by Amazon Fulfillment
Poland Sp. z o.o., Wrocław